ARAB ARAB ALL YEAR LONG!

illustrated by

Cathy Camper Sawsan Chalabi

CANDLEWICK PRESS

In our houses,
on the sidewalk,
in the country,
and downtown,

we're exploring, sharing,
making things
all year round.

Wrapping
grape leaves,
playing doumbek,
drawing henna tattoos,

we're Arab, Arab, Arab,
the whole year
through!

JANUARY

يد الجوزاء   الدبران

رجل

At midnight on New Year's Eve, we go outside to see the sky. It's our family tradition to find the stars with Arabic names and make a New Year's wish.

Aldebaran, Rigel, Betelgeuse . . .

The stars wink back at us across the centuries
on the first night of this brand-new year.

FEBRUARY

We love comics! Geddo says that a comic about
Martin Luther King Jr. that was translated into
Arabic and Farsi might have even inspired some
people to protest in the Egyptian revolution.

We decide that we're going to make a comic to spark change at our school, too, teaching our classmates about Muslims and Ramadan.

Now our friends will know how to wish us Eid Mubarak!

MARCH

For work or school, you must be prompt! But when we're gathering for fun, it's OK to show up on Arab Time. Come one hour or even two hours late to share meze, laugh out loud, and talk, talk, talk!

Maybe Arabs show up late because our Arab goodbyes stretch so long into the night.

APRIL

I love baking with Sitti! At Easter I help her make maamoul. I mix the dough and we make four kinds of fillings: walnut, pistachio, date, and fig. Sitti forms a ball of dough into a little cup, puts some filling inside, and pinches the dough to cover it up.

We press the maamoul into the molds to make a special design on top, then bake them until they're golden. The design on each maamoul tells you what's inside!

I'm learning to write Arabic. The vowels are dots and dashes, hovering like birds around the consonants. Arabic reads from right to left, perfect for a left-hander like me. Now my hand won't smear my words.

JUNE

We race up and down the alleys scouting for wild grapevines that cover fences and garages in waterfalls of green. We fill up our bags with tender leaves the size of our hands.

Later, we help our moms
and aunties roll them up.

Warak enab for supper!

JULY

The heat of summer reminds Mom of Morocco,
and of the scents where she grew up.

For her birthday, we made a special perfume, mixing jasmine and honeysuckle with tangerine, lemon, and mint essential oils. We added Moroccan spices, too: cayenne, turmeric, cinnamon, and ginger, plus lots of fresh ground pepper.

Mom says she'll treasure it forever as a memory of her home—and us!

AUGUST

My father's band plays at the Arab Summer Festival. His doumbek makes different sounds.

DOUM!
His flat hand sounds through the center of the drum.

TAK!
His right middle fingers slap the drum skin's edge.

KA! KA! KA!
His left middle fingers reply like fast raindrops of sound.

And when my dad warms the drumhead over the fire, sometimes the doumbek speaks by itself:

POP-POW!

SEPTEMBER

We look online at hijab fashion sites for days, planning ideas for our costumes.

At our local comic convention, we are sailors, singers, vampires, and superheroes. And I win a prize for my costume of Egyptian singer Umm Kulthum!

OCTOBER

Mom has pomegranates!
Yallah, yallah, into the tub!
We'll eat them there so we
can be as messy as we want!

NOVEMBER

When days grow dark and cold winds blow strong,
I wear my keffiyeh to keep my memories warm.

DECEMBER

My school friends are busy celebrating winter holidays. Mom lets me have a slumber party instead.

My big sister is the best henna artist; all my cousins want her designs. We wrap our hands in gauze and watch horror movies in the dark at our henna party sleepover!

The henna dries while we're asleep. The next day when we rub the dried paste away, delicate designs adorn our palms.

Looking up at stars,
or skateboarding in the sun,

or waiting for the bus
with our headphones on,

no matter where we are,
no matter what we do,

we're Arab, Arab, Arab,
the whole year through!

NOTES AND GLOSSARY

ARAB ASTRONOMY: Arabs have observed the skies, named stars, and used stars for navigation for centuries. At a time when Europe was in the Dark Ages, the ninth to fifteenth centuries were the Golden Age of Islamic-Arab astronomy, and knowledge eventually spread west, helping foster the European Renaissance of science. Most of the Arabic star names can be traced back to al-Sufi, a tenth-century astronomer who was born in Persia but wrote in Arabic.

ARAB SPRING: a series of revolutions, demonstrations, and protests that swept across the Arab world, beginning in December 2010 in Tunisia and spreading to Egypt, Libya, Syria, Yemen, and Bahrain, inspiring street demonstrations and protests in countries around the world. The 1957–1958 comic *Martin Luther King and the Montgomery Story* was translated into Farsi and Arabic half a century later and distributed in print and online. The comic offers advice on nonviolent resistance, and it is thought that some of these strategies were used in the 2011 Egyptian Revolution.

DOUMBEK: a ceramic or metal drum with a skin or synthetic head. The drum is often held in the crook of one's arm and played with hand strikes and finger rolls. Drumheads made of skin are like barometers; when the weather is humid, they are loose, and their tone is low and dull, but in dry, hot weather, or when held over the dry heat of a fire, the skin tightens for a higher, sharper tone—and sometimes even pops.

EID MUBARAK!: a way Muslims wish each other well for the two holidays of Eid al-Adha (which recognizes God's test of Ibrahim and also marks the culmination of the annual Hajj pilgrimage to Mecca) and Eid al-Fitr (which marks the end of Ramadan). It means *Have a blessed feast*.

GEDDO: one way to say *grandfather* in Arabic

HENNA: a plant-based dye, usually reddish orange or black, used throughout the Middle East and parts of Africa to create intricate, temporary tattoo-like designs, usually on hands or feet.

HIJAB: In the Quran, the Islamic sacred book, God advises both male and female Muslims to dress modestly, and this principle is called hijab. There are many stylish and high-fashion designs for Muslim women's wear.

KEFFIYEH: a square scarf worn in the Middle East to protect the head from sun and dust. Throughout the Arab diaspora, Arabs wear keffiyehs as a way of representing Arab culture, as a fashion statement, and as a symbol of solidarity with the nation of Palestine.

MAAMOUL: a sweet, cookie-like pastry made of dough filled with different mixtures. They are often flavored with rose or orange blossom water and mahlab, a spice made of ground cherry pits. The dough can be decorated by hand or by pressing the pastry into a mold before baking. Muslims eat them at Eid al-Fitr and Eid al-Adha, and Christians eat them on Easter, but people also enjoy eating them any time during the year.

MEZE: a word used in Mediterranean countries to refer to an appetizer or a meal of appetizers

POMEGRANATE: a round red fruit filled with many small seeds, each surrounded by a sweet juice sac. Pomegranates ripen in the fall, and eating them is always messy!

SITTI: one way to say *grandmother* in Arabic

UMM KULTHUM: an iconic, internationally famous Muslim Egyptian singer who has sold more than 80 million records worldwide. Her signature look included sunglasses and a turban.

WARAK ENAB: grape leaves stuffed with a mixture of rice, lamb, and spices, such as cinnamon. Stuffed grape leaves and cabbage leaves are popular throughout the Mediterranean; there are many variations, including vegetarian recipes, and they may be served hot or cold.

YALLAH: Arabic for *Come here! Come on!*

AUTHOR'S NOTE

Thank you to Hannah Moushabeck and Aysha Ghazoul for your support and for sharing your family stories with me. Many thanks and gratitude to Kathy Haddad, Nadia Phelps, Lana Barkawi, Nahid Khan, Linda Dalal Sawaya, Rima Karami, Mariam Habib, and Jennifer Camper for your wisdom, support, advice, and friendship. Much gratitude to my editor Andrea Tompa and all the folks at Candlewick, to my agent Jennifer Laughran, and to Sawsan Chalabi for her amazing art!

This calendar of stories is based on events from my own life, stories Arab friends shared with me, and other tales inspired by real-life events. They're meant to show the rich culture and the blend of old and new that exists throughout the Arab diaspora.

There is no universal definition of who is Arab. Broadly speaking, Arabs' families come from the Middle East or northern Africa. They often speak Arabic and they have some cultural and ethnic traits in common. However, not all people from this part of the world identify as Arab, and even among Arabs, there are many variations in language, culture, and ethnicity. There are also political reasons why someone may or may not identify as Arab, and Western representations often differ from how Arabs view themselves. Note that I have used the term "Middle East" in this book as it is the most common and recognizable way to refer to this region, but that term is problematic, as it was created by colonial countries and doesn't include northern Africa. The English-language acronyms SWANA (Southwest Asia and North Africa) and MENA (Middle East and North Africa) are sometimes used instead.

The Arab League currently recognizes twenty-two Arab states: Algeria, Bahrain, Comoros, Djibouti, Egypt, Iraq, Jordan, Kuwait, Lebanon, Libya, Mauritania, Morocco, Oman, Palestine, Qatar, Saudi Arabia, Somalia, Sudan, Syria, Tunisia, United Arab Emirates, and Yemen. But the Arab diaspora is worldwide, including both immigrants and Arabs born outside of Arab countries. Arabs can be of many religions, primarily Muslim and Christian, and they can also be nonreligious.

First edition 2022

Library of Congress Catalog Card Number 2021947147
ISBN 978-1-5362-1395-9

APS 27 26 25 24 23 22
10 9 8 7 6 5 4 3 2 1

Printed in Humen, Dongguan, China

This book was typeset in Blue Sheep.
The illustrations were created digitally.

Candlewick Press
99 Dover Street
Somerville, Massachusetts 02144

www.candlewick.com

For my family, and for Arabs, Arabs everywhere!
CC

For my dad, Abdul-Fattah. Thank you, Baba, for your wisdom, unconditional love, and for raising us to know our culture. I am so proud to be your daughter.
SC